A gift for

_____

From

_____

Date

_____

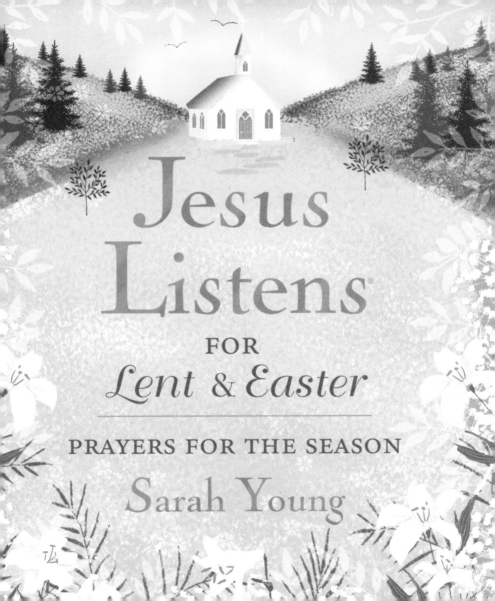

Jesus Listens

FOR
Lent & Easter

PRAYERS FOR THE SEASON

Sarah Young

Jesus Listens™ for Lent and Easter

© 2025 Jesus Calling Foundation

The content from this book has been excerpted from *Jesus Listens* © 2021 Sarah Young and from *Jesus Calling* © 2004 Sarah Young.

Published in Nashville, Tennessee, by Thomas Nelson. Thomas Nelson is a registered trademark of HarperCollins Christian Publishing, Inc.

Art by Sally Wilson

Thomas Nelson titles may be purchased in bulk for educational, business, fund-raising, or sales promotional use. For information, please email SpecialMarkets@ThomasNelson.com.

Unless otherwise noted, Scripture quotations are taken from The Holy Bible, New International Version , NIV . Copyright © 1973, 1978, 1984 by Biblica, Inc. Used by permission of Zondervan. All rights reserved worldwide. www. Zondervan. com. The "NIV" and "New International Version" are trademarks registered in the United States Patent and Trademark Office by Biblica, Inc.

Scripture quotations marked AMP are taken from the Amplified Bible (AMP). Copyright © 2015 by The Lockman Foundation. Used by permission. www.Lockman.org

Scripture quotations marked AMPC are taken from the Amplified Bible, Classic Edition (AMPC). Copyright © 1954, 1958, 1962, 1964, 1965, 1987 by The Lockman Foundation. Used by permission. www.Lockman.org

Scripture quotations marked ESV are taken from the ESV Bible (The Holy Bible, English Standard Version). Copyright © 2001 by Crossway, a publishing ministry of Good News Publishers. Used by permission. All rights reserved.

Scripture quotations marked HCSB are taken from the Holman Christian Standard Bible Copyright © 1999, 2000, 2002, 2003, 2009 by Holman Bible Publishers. Used by permission. HCSB° is a federally registered trademark of Holman Bible Publishers.

Scripture quotations marked NASB 1995 are taken from the New American Standard Bible (NASB). Copyright © 1960, 1962, 1963, 1968, 1971, 1972, 1973, 1975, 1977, 1995 by The Lockman Foundation. Used by permission. www.Lockman.org

Scripture quotations marked NASB are taken from the New American Standard Bible° (NASB). Copyright © 1960, 1962, 1963, 1968, 1971, 1972, 1973, 1975, 1977, 1995, 2020 by The Lockman Foundation. Used by permission. www.Lockman.org

Scripture quotations marked NET are taken from the NET Bible copyright ©1996–2017 by Biblical Studies Press, L.L.C. http://netbible.com. All rights reserved.

Scripture quotations marked NKJV are taken from the New King James Version . Copyright © 1982 by Thomas Nelson. Used by permission. All rights reserved.

Scripture quotations marked NLT are taken from the Holy Bible, New Living Translation. © 1996, 2004, 2015 by Tyndale House Foundation. Used by permission of Tyndale House Ministries, Carol Stream, Illinois 60188. All rights reserved.

The Scripture quotations marked NRSV are taken from the New Revised Standard Version Bible. Copyright © 1989 National Council of the Churches of Christ in the United States of America. Used by permission. All rights reserved worldwide.

ISBN 978-1-4002-5087-5 (HC)
ISBN 978-1-4002-5089-9 (audiobook)
ISBN 978-1-4002-5084-4 (eBook)

Printed in Malaysia

25 26 27 28 29 SEM 10 9 8 7 6 5 4 3 2 1

BLESSED SAVIOR,

Thank You for the glorious gift of grace! Your Word teaches that *by grace I have been saved through faith. And this is not my own doing; it's not a result of my works.* Even the faith I needed to believe in You—to receive salvation—is a gift from You. Through Your work on the cross, I've been given the astonishing blessing of *eternal Life.* Help me respond to Your amazing generosity with a grateful heart. I can never thank You too fervently or too frequently for grace.

During this Lenten season, I want to take time to ponder what it means to have all my sins forgiven. I am no longer on a pathway to hell; my ultimate destination is *a new heaven and a new earth.* This guaranteed heavenly inheritance gives me a great reason to rejoice every day of my life.

As I walk with You today, I'll try to thank You often for the matchless gift of grace. I pray that my gratitude for grace may increase my awareness of the many *other* blessings You provide—making me even *more* thankful.

IN YOUR GRACIOUS NAME, JESUS, AMEN.

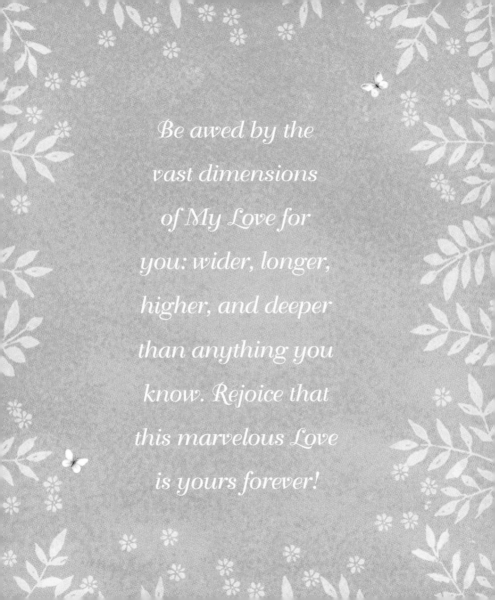

Be awed by the
vast dimensions
of My Love for
you: wider, longer,
higher, and deeper
than anything you
know. Rejoice that
this marvelous Love
is yours forever!

By grace you have been saved through faith. And
this is not your own doing; it is the gift of God, not
a result of works, so that no one may boast.

EPHESIANS 2:8–9 ESV

"God so loved the world that he gave his one
and only Son, that whoever believes in him
shall not perish but have eternal life."

JOHN 3:16

Now I saw a new heaven and a new earth, for the
first heaven and the first earth had passed away.

REVELATION 21:1 NKJV

Gracious Lord,

Help me to *hope for what I do not see—eagerly waiting for it with perseverance.* Among the five senses, sight is the one I value the most. You created the world gloriously beautiful, and I delight in seeing the beauty of Your creation. However, I realize that hope, which is itself a kind of vision, is even more wonderful than sight. Hope enables me to see—through the eyes of my heart—things that are *not yet.* The most stunning example of this is the hope of heaven. Your Word tells me that my ultimate destination is to share in Your Glory! I can trust in this magnificent promise because it's based on Your work on the cross and Your miraculous resurrection.

I need to practice hoping for things I do not see—both for this life and the next. Please guide me into hopes and dreams that are in line with Your will. I want to train the eyes of my heart to "see" these blessings while praying for Your will to be done fully and only. Teach me to *wait eagerly with perseverance*—with my focus primarily on *You* but also on the longed-for outcome. You are my Hope!

In Your great Name, Jesus, amen.

Find fulfillment through living close to Me, yielding to My purposes for you. Though I may lead you along paths that feel alien to you, trust that I know what I am doing. If you follow Me wholeheartedly, you will discover facets of yourself that were previously hidden.

If we hope for what we do not see, we
eagerly wait for it with perseverance.

ROMANS 8:25 NKJV

"The glory which You gave Me I have given them,
that they may be one just as We are one."

JOHN 17:22 NKJV

Now faith is the assurance (the confirmation,
the title deed) of the things [we] hope for, being
the proof of things [we] do not see *and* the
conviction of their reality [faith perceiving as
real fact what is not revealed to the senses].

HEBREWS 11:1 AMPC

Precious Savior,

I rejoice and exult in hope! I have good reason to be joyful because I'm on my way to heaven. Thank You, Lord, for paying the penalty for all my sins and for clothing me in Your own righteousness. *This* is the basis of my hope—a hope that is secure, regardless of my circumstances. *No one can snatch me out of Your hand.* In You I have absolute, eternal security!

Your Word instructs me to *be constant in prayer.* I need this communication with You at all times, but especially when I'm struggling. Yet during trials, my ability to focus on You can be hampered by stress and fatigue. So I'm grateful for the amazing source of strength I have within me: Your Holy Spirit. As I ask Your Spirit to *control my mind,* He strengthens me and enables me to pray. I'm glad that my prayers don't have to be eloquent or organized; I can just let them flow freely out of my circumstances.

Lord, please help me stay in communication with You, especially during times of adversity—so that I can *be steadfast and patient in suffering.*

In Your hopeful Name, Jesus, amen.

Rest in Me, My child.
This time devoted to
Me is meant to be
peaceful, not stressful.
You don't have to
perform in order
to receive My Love.
I have boundless,
unconditional
Love for you.

Rejoice *and* exult in hope; be steadfast and patient in suffering *and* tribulation; be constant in prayer.

ROMANS 12:12 AMPC

"I give them eternal life, and they will never perish—ever! No one will snatch them out of My hand."

JOHN 10:28 HCSB

The mind of sinful man is death, but the mind controlled by the Spirit is life and peace.

ROMANS 8:6

PRECIOUS JESUS,

You are the Resurrection and the Life. Whoever believes in You will live, even though he dies. You spoke this powerful truth to Martha when her brother Lazarus had been dead for four days, and she believed You. Then You commanded Lazarus to come out of his tomb, and he did!

I love pondering Your teaching that *You are the Way, the Truth, and the Life.* You are everything I could ever need—for this life and the next. *All the treasures of wisdom and knowledge are hidden in You.* Believing this truth simplifies my life and helps me stay focused on You. Please train me in the joyful discipline of treasuring You above all else.

You are the answer to all my struggles, the Joy that pervades all time and circumstances. You make my hard times bearable and my good times even better. So I *come to You* just as I am, desiring to share more and more of my life with You. I rejoice as I journey with You—*the Way* who guides me step by step and *the Resurrection* who gives me eternal Life.

IN YOUR MAJESTIC NAME, AMEN.

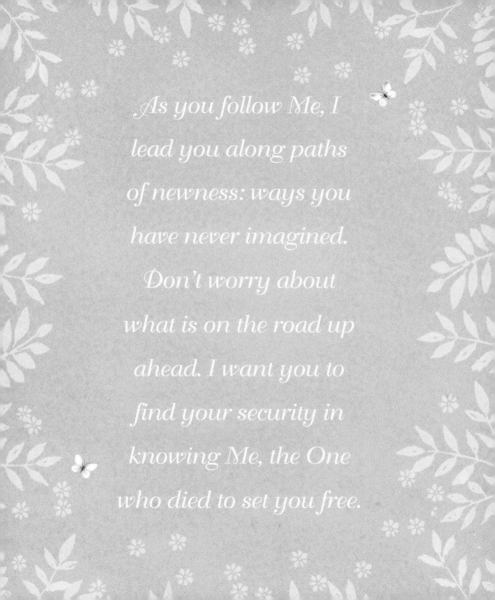

As you follow Me, I lead you along paths of newness: ways you have never imagined. Don't worry about what is on the road up ahead. I want you to find your security in knowing Me, the One who died to set you free.

"I am the resurrection and the life. He who
believes in me will live, even though he dies."

JOHN 11:25

Jesus said to him, "I am the way, the truth, and the life.
No one comes to the Father except through Me."

JOHN 14:6 NKJV

My purpose is that . . . they may have the full riches
of complete understanding, in order that they may
know the mystery of God, namely, Christ, in whom are
hidden all the treasures of wisdom and knowledge.

COLOSSIANS 2:2–3

GOD, MY REFUGE,

Help me *not to dwell on the past*. I can learn from the past, but I don't want it to be my focus. I know I cannot undo things that have already occurred, no matter how hard I try. So I come to You and *pour out my heart*—remembering that *You are my refuge*, worthy of my trust *at all times*.

One way I can build up my confidence in You is to tell You frequently: "I trust You, Lord." Speaking these affirmations of trust brightens my day immensely—blowing away dark clouds of worry.

You are always *doing a new thing!* So I'll be on the lookout for all that You're accomplishing in my life. Please open the eyes of my mind and heart so I can see the many opportunities You've placed along my path. And protect me from falling into such a routine way of living that I see only the same old things—missing the newness.

I'm learning that You can make a way where there appears to be no way. *With You all things are possible!*

IN YOUR AMAZING NAME, JESUS, AMEN.

Come to Me with
a teachable spirit,
eager to be changed.
A close walk with
Me is a life of
continual newness.

"Forget the former things; do not dwell on the past. See, I am doing a new thing! Now it springs up; do you not perceive it? I am making a way in the desert and streams in the wasteland."

Isaiah 43:18–19

Trust in him at all times, O people; pour out your hearts to him, for God is our refuge.

Psalm 62:8

Jesus said to them, "With people this is impossible, but with God all things are possible."

Matthew 19:26 nasb

DEAR JESUS,

Help me remember that I am *not* on trial. Your Word assures me *there is no condemnation for those who belong to You*—those who know You as Savior. I have already been judged "Not guilty!" in the courts of heaven through Your work on the cross. Your sacrificial death and miraculous resurrection set me free from bondage to sin. I want to live joyfully in this freedom—learning to relax and savor my guilt-free position in Your kingdom. Yet I struggle to live in this amazing freedom You won for me, Lord.

I'm so thankful for the grace You have *lavished on me*. Please work in my heart so that gratitude for Your grace fuels my desire to live according to Your will. The closer I live to You, the better I can discern Your will—and the more fully I can experience Your Joy and Peace. Knowing You intimately helps me trust You enough to receive Your Peace even in the midst of trouble. And *overflowing with thankfulness* has the delightful "side effect" of increasing my Joy!

IN YOUR GRACIOUS NAME, AMEN.

When I unburden you, you are undeniably free! Stand up straight and tall in My Presence so that no one can place more burdens on your back. Look into My Face and feel the warmth of My Love-Light shining upon you. It is this unconditional Love that frees you from both fears and sins.

"If the Son sets you free, you will be free indeed."

John 8:36 esv

In him we have redemption through his blood,
the forgiveness of sins, in accordance with
the riches of God's grace that he lavished on
us with all wisdom and understanding.

Ephesians 1:7–8

Just as you received Christ Jesus as Lord,
continue to live in him, rooted and built up
in him, strengthened in the faith as you were
taught, and overflowing with thankfulness.

Colossians 2:6–7

MY SAVIOR-KING,

Thank You for Your precious *robe of righteousness* that covers me from head to toe. The price You paid for this glorious garment was astronomical—Your own sacred blood. I realize I could *never* purchase this royal robe, no matter how hard I work. So I'm extremely grateful that Your righteousness is a free gift! If I forget this amazing truth, I feel ill at ease in my regal robe. Sometimes I even squirm under the velvety fabric as if it were made of scratchy sackcloth.

Lord, I long to trust You enough to remember my privileged position in Your kingdom—and to relax in the luxuriant folds of my magnificent robe. I need to keep my eyes on *You* as I practice walking in this *garment of salvation*.

When my behavior is unfitting for a child of the King, it's tempting to try to throw off my royal robe. Help me instead to throw off the unrighteous behavior! Then I'll be able to feel at ease in this garment of grace, enjoying the gift You fashioned for me before the creation of the world.

IN YOUR REGAL NAME, JESUS, AMEN.

My own children have nothing to fear, for I have cleansed them by My blood and clothed them in My righteousness. Be blessed by My intimate nearness. Since I live in you, let Me also live through you, shining My Light into the darkness.

I will rejoice greatly in the LORD . . . for He has clothed me
with garments of salvation, He has wrapped me with a
robe of righteousness, as a bridegroom decks himself with
a garland, and as a bride adorns herself with her jewels.

ISAIAH 61:10 NASB 1995

God made him who had no sin to be sin for us, so that
in him we might become the righteousness of God.

2 CORINTHIANS 5:21

You were taught, with regard to your former way of
life, to put off your old self . . . ; to be made new in the
attitude of your minds; and to put on the new self, created
to be like God in true righteousness and holiness.

EPHESIANS 4:22–24

TRIUMPHANT GOD,

Your Word poses the rhetorical question: *"If God is for us, who can be against us?"* I trust that You are indeed *for me* since I am Your follower. I realize this verse does not mean that no one will ever oppose me. It does mean that having *You* on my side is the most important fact of my existence.

Regardless of what losses I experience, I am on the winning side. You won the decisive victory through Your death and resurrection! You are the eternal Victor, and I share in Your triumph because I belong to You forever. No matter how much adversity I encounter on my journey to heaven, nothing can ultimately prevail against me!

Knowing that my future is utterly secure is changing my perspective dramatically. Instead of living in defensive mode—striving to protect myself from suffering—I am learning to follow You confidently, wherever You lead. You are teaching me not only to *seek Your Face* and follow Your lead but to enjoy this adventure of abandoning myself to You. I rejoice that You are with me continually and *You are always ready to help me in times of trouble.*

IN YOUR MAGNIFICENT NAME, JESUS, AMEN.

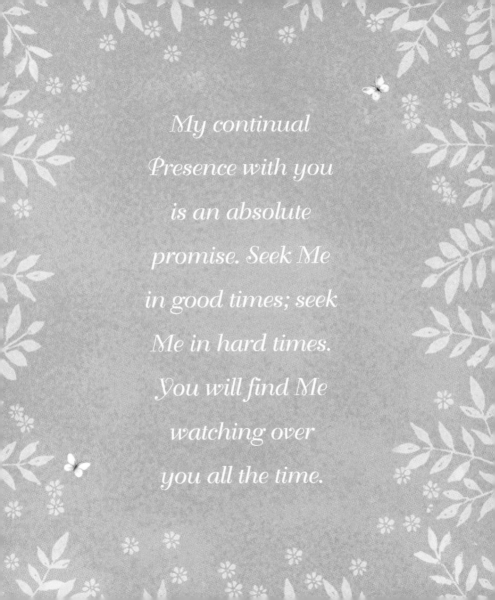

My continual
Presence with you
is an absolute
promise. Seek Me
in good times; seek
Me in hard times.
You will find Me
watching over
you all the time.

What, then, shall we say in response to this?
If God is for us, who can be against us?

Romans 8:31

When You said, "Seek My face," my heart said
to You, "Your face, Lord, I will seek."

Psalm 27:8 nkjv

God is our refuge and strength, always
ready to help in times of trouble.

Psalm 46:1 nlt

Invincible Jesus,

Your Love has conquered me and *set me free!* The Power of Your Love is so great that it has enslaved me to You. *I am not my own; I was bought with a price*—Your holy blood. Because of Your amazing sacrifice for me, I want to serve You with every fiber of my being. I know that my service is woefully inadequate. Nonetheless, when I yield myself to Your will, You bless me with Joy.

Because You are perfect in all Your ways, I can give myself wholeheartedly to You without fear that You might take advantage of me. Actually, being conquered by You protects me and makes me truly free. You have invaded the innermost core of my being, and Your Spirit is taking over more and more territory within me. As Your Word teaches, *where the Spirit of the Lord is, there is freedom*. I rejoice in the freedom I have found in You, Jesus. And I surrender gladly to Your conquering Love!

In Your powerful, loving Name, amen.

Do not fear change, for I am making you a new creation, with old things passing away and new things continually on the horizon. When you cling to old ways and sameness, you resist My work within you. I want you to embrace all that I am doing in your life, finding your security in Me alone.

Thanks be to God that, though you used to be slaves to sin, you have come to obey from your heart the pattern of teaching that has now claimed your allegiance. You have been set free from sin and have become slaves to righteousness.

ROMANS 6:17–18

Do you not know that your body is a temple of the Holy Spirit within you, whom you have from God? You are not your own, for you were bought with a price. So glorify God in your body.

1 CORINTHIANS 6:19–20 ESV

Now the Lord is the Spirit, and where the Spirit of the Lord is, there is freedom.

2 CORINTHIANS 3:17

Compassionate Lord,

Your Word tells me *You broaden the path beneath me so that my ankles do not turn*. This shows me how intricately You are involved in my life-journey. You know exactly what is ahead of me, and You can alter the hazardous parts of my path before I get there—making my way easier. Sometimes You enable me to see what You have done on my behalf. At other times You spare me hardships without showing me Your protective work. Either way, Your watchful work on my behalf demonstrates Your loving involvement in my life.

From my limited human perspective, Your ways are often mysterious. You do not protect me—or anyone—from *all* adversity. Neither were *You* shielded from hardship during Your thirty-three years of living in this world. On the contrary, You willingly suffered unimaginable pain, humiliation, and agony on the cross—for my sake! When Your Father turned away from You, You experienced unspeakable suffering. But because You were willing to endure that excruciating isolation from Him, I *never* have to suffer alone. Please help me to remember and rejoice in the glorious truth that *You are with me always*—and be thankful!

In Your marvelous Name, Jesus, amen.

My Presence watches over you continually, protecting you from both known and unknown dangers. Entrust yourself to My watch-care, which is the best security system available. I am with you and will watch over you wherever you go.

You broaden the path beneath me,
so that my ankles do not turn.

PSALM 18:36

He will not let your foot slip—he who
watches over you will not slumber.

PSALM 121:3

About the ninth hour Jesus cried out with a loud
voice, saying, "Eli, Eli, lama sabachthani?" that is,
"My God, My God, why have You forsaken Me?"

MATTHEW 27:46 NKJV

CHERISHED LORD JESUS,

While I sit quietly in Your Presence, please fill my heart and mind with thankfulness. This is a most delightful way to spend time with You. When my mind needs a focal point, I can gaze at Your Love poured out for me on the cross. I need to remember that *neither height nor depth nor anything else in all creation can separate me from Your Love*. This remembrance builds a foundation of gratitude in me—a foundation that circumstances cannot shake.

As I go through this day, I want to find all the treasures You have placed along my way. I know that You lovingly go before me and plant little pleasures to brighten my day. I'll look carefully for these blessings and pluck them one by one. Then when I reach the end of the day, I will have gathered a lovely bouquet. I'll offer it up to You, Lord, with gratitude in my heart. As I lie down to sleep, help me relax in Your Presence and receive Your Peace—with thankful thoughts playing a lullaby in my mind.

IN YOUR SOOTHING NAME, AMEN.

Thankfulness enables you to see the abundance I shower upon you daily. Your prayers and petitions are winged into heaven's throne room when they are permeated with thanksgiving.

Neither height nor depth, nor anything else in all creation, will be able to separate us from the love of God that is in Christ Jesus our Lord.

ROMANS 8:39

No one can lay any foundation other than the one already laid, which is Jesus Christ.

1 CORINTHIANS 3:11

You have filled my heart with greater joy than when their grain and new wine abound. I will lie down and sleep in peace, for you alone, O LORD, make me dwell in safety.

PSALM 4:7–8

DELIGHTFUL JESUS,

Thank You for showing me that heaven is both present and future. As I walk along my life-path holding Your hand, I am already in touch with the essence of heaven—nearness to You! While journeying with You, I perceive lovely hints of heaven. The earth is radiantly alive with Your Presence. Shimmering sunshine awakens my heart, gently reminding me of Your brilliant Light. Birds and flowers, trees and skies evoke praises to Your holy Name. Help me to be fully open to the splendors of Your creation as I walk in the Light of Your Love.

Thanks to Your sacrifice, I rejoice that there's an entrance to heaven at the end of my journey. Only *You* know when I'll reach that destination, but I trust that You're preparing me for it each step of the way. The absolute assurance of my forever-home *fills me with Joy and Peace*. I know I'll arrive at this glorious haven in Your perfect timing—not one moment too soon or too late. While I walk with You down *the path of life*, the sure hope of heaven strengthens and encourages me!

IN YOUR HEAVENLY NAME, AMEN.

Open wide your heart and mind to receive more and more of Me. When your Joy in Me meets My Joy in you, there are fireworks of heavenly ecstasy. This is eternal life here and now: a tiny foretaste of what awaits you in the life to come.

For as in Adam all die, so in Christ
all will be made alive.

1 CORINTHIANS 15:22

We have this hope as an anchor
for the soul, firm and secure.

HEBREWS 6:19

May the God of hope fill you with all
joy and peace as you trust in him, so
that you may overflow with hope by
the power of the Holy Spirit.

ROMANS 15:13

My great, loving God,

You are my living Lord, *my Rock*, my Savior-God! Help me to spend ample time with You—pondering Your greatness and Your endless commitment to me. I live in a culture where so many people are leery of making commitments. Even those who say "I do" often change their minds later and leave. You, however, are my forever-Friend and the eternal Lover of my soul. I am utterly secure in Your Love!

Instead of focusing on troubles in my life and in the world, I want to think more about who You are. Not only are You my living Lord and unchanging Rock; You are *God my Savior.* Your death on the cross for my sins *saves me to the uttermost* because You are *eternal God.* I don't need to worry that You will stop loving me if my performance isn't good enough—it's *Your* goodness and *Your* righteousness that keep me secure in Your Love. Your unending commitment to me strengthens and comforts me as I journey through this trouble-filled world. And I eagerly await the time when I will live with You in Glory!

In Your breathtaking Name, Jesus, amen.

I love you with an everlasting Love, which flows out from the depths of eternity. Before you were born, I knew you. Ponder the awesome mystery of a Love that encompasses you from before birth to beyond the grave.

The Lord lives! Praise be to my Rock!
Exalted be God my Savior!

PSALM 18:46

He is also able to save to the uttermost
those who come to God through Him.

HEBREWS 7:25 NKJV

The eternal God is your refuge, and underneath
are the everlasting arms. He will drive out your
enemy before you, saying, "Destroy him!"

DEUTERONOMY 33:27

BELOVED JESUS,

Your Word invites me to *taste and see that You are good*. I've discovered that the more fully I experience You, the more convinced I become of Your goodness. I rejoice that You are *the living One who sees me* and participates in every aspect of my life. You're training me to seek You in each moment, letting Your Love flow through me into the lives of others. Sometimes Your blessings come to me in mysterious ways—through pain and trouble. At such times I can know Your goodness only through my trust in You. My understanding fails me time after time, but trust keeps me close to You.

I thank You for the gift of Your Peace—a gift of such immense proportions that I can't begin to fathom its depth or breadth. When You appeared to Your disciples after Your resurrection, it was Peace that You communicated first of all. They desperately needed Your Peace—to calm their fears and clear their minds. You also speak Peace to me, for You know my anxious thoughts. Please help me tune out other voices so I can hear You more clearly. Lord, I come to You with open hands and an open heart, ready to receive Your Peace.

IN YOUR PEACEFUL NAME, AMEN.

Seek My Face, and I
will share My mind
with you, opening your
eyes to see things from
My perspective. Do
not let your heart be
troubled, and do not be
afraid. The Peace I give
is sufficient for you.

Taste and see that the LORD is good;
blessed is the man who takes refuge in him.

PSALM 34:8

On the evening of that first day of the week,
when the disciples were together, with the doors
locked for fear of the Jews, Jesus came and stood
among them and said, "Peace be with you!"

JOHN 20:19

Let the peace of Christ rule in your hearts,
since as members of one body you were
called to peace. And be thankful.

COLOSSIANS 3:15

MY STRONG SAVIOR,

Help me *not to grow weary or lose heart*. When I'm dealing with difficulties that go on and on, it's easy to get so tired that I feel like giving up. Chronic problems tend to wear me out and wear me down. But I realize that if I focus too much on my troubles, I'm in danger of sliding into a black hole of self-pity or despair.

Unrelieved physical tiredness can make me vulnerable to emotional exhaustion and spiritual fatigue—*losing heart*. Thank You for equipping me to transcend my troubles by *fixing my eyes on You*. I know that You paid a terrible price to be my living Savior—*enduring the cross*. When I contemplate Your willingness to suffer so much for me, I gain strength to endure my own hardships.

I've found that worshiping You is a delightful way of renewing my strength! When I take steps of faith by praising You in the midst of adversity, Your glorious Light shines upon me. I ask that this Light may reflect to others as I live close to You, aware of Your loving Presence. And I rejoice that I am *being transformed into Your likeness with ever-increasing Glory!*

IN YOUR BEAUTIFUL NAME, JESUS, AMEN.

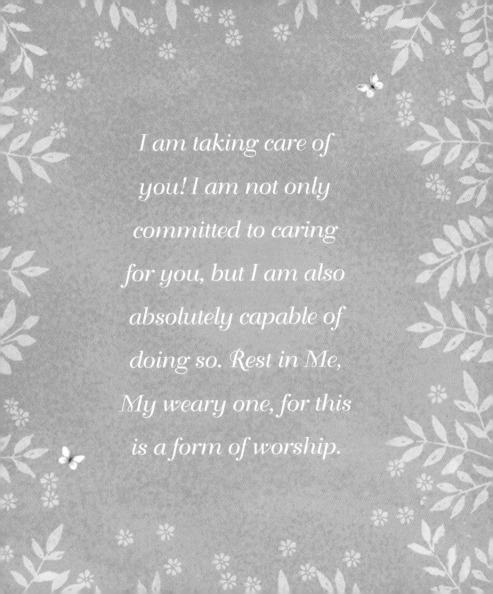

I am taking care of you! I am not only committed to caring for you, but I am also absolutely capable of doing so. Rest in Me, My weary one, for this is a form of worship.

PEACE

Let us fix our eyes on Jesus . . . who for the joy
set before him endured the cross, scorning
its shame, and sat down at the right hand of
the throne of God. Consider him who endured
such opposition from sinful men, so that
you will not grow weary and lose heart.

HEBREWS 12:2–3

We walk by faith, not by sight.

2 CORINTHIANS 5:7 NKJV

We, who with unveiled faces all reflect the
Lord's glory, are being transformed into his
likeness with ever-increasing glory, which
comes from the Lord, who is the Spirit.

2 CORINTHIANS 3:18

Gracious Jesus,

From Your fullness I have received grace upon grace. I worship You as I ponder Your astonishing gift of salvation—*by grace through faith* in You. Because it's entirely a gift, *not a result of works*, my salvation is absolutely secure! My part was just to receive this precious gift—believing with the faith that You provided. I rejoice in this infinitely costly treasure, bought with the price of Your blood.

I've found that multiple blessings flow out of Your wondrous grace. My guilt feelings melt away in the warm Light of Your forgiveness. My identity as a *child of God* gives my life meaning and purpose. My relationships with other people improve as I relate to them with the love and forgiveness You've given me.

O Lord, fill my heart with overflowing gratitude as I ponder Your glorious grace. Please remind me to spend time thinking about and thanking You for the bountiful blessings in my life. This protects my heart from the weeds of ingratitude that spring up so easily. Teach me to *be thankful*!

In Your merciful Name, amen.

I view you through eyes of grace, so don't be afraid of My intimate awareness. Allow the Light of My healing Presence to shine into the deepest recesses of your being—cleansing, healing, refreshing, and renewing you.

From his fullness we have all
received, grace upon grace.

JOHN 1:16 ESV

Yet to all who received him, to those who believed in
his name, he gave the right to become children of God.

JOHN 1:12

Since we are receiving a kingdom that cannot
be shaken, let us be thankful, and so worship
God acceptably with reverence and awe.

HEBREWS 12:28

MERCIFUL GOD,

Your steadfast Love never ceases, Your mercies never come to an end; they are new every morning. I desperately want to rest in this truth, but I'm struggling to do so. Today, the only things that seem endless are my problems and my pain. Yet I know You are *here*—tenderly present—ready to help me get safely through this day. Your loving Presence is my lifeline that keeps me from giving up in despair.

On some days, when things are going well, I readily trust in Your steadfast Love. But when new, unexpected problems arise, trusting You takes much more effort. At such times, I need to remember that Your ever-new mercies far outweigh my difficulties. *Great is Your faithfulness!*

While I'm dressing, I like to remind myself that *You have clothed me in garments of salvation.* Because I wear Your *robe of righteousness,* I am on my way to heaven! This is an incredible act of mercy—snatching me from the jaws of hell and putting me on the path to Glory. Nothing I face today can compare with Your amazing gift of *eternal Life!*

IN YOUR VICTORIOUS NAME, JESUS, AMEN.

You can turn to Me at any point, and I will help you crawl out of the mire of discouragement. I will infuse My strength into you moment by moment, giving you all that you need for this day. Trust Me by relying on My empowering Presence.

HOPE

The steadfast love of the LORD never ceases,
his mercies never come to an end; they are new
every morning; great is your faithfulness.

LAMENTATIONS 3:22–23 NRSV

I will greatly rejoice in the LORD, my soul
shall be joyful in my God; for He has clothed
me with the garments of salvation.

ISAIAH 61:10 NKJV

"God so loved the world, that he gave his only
Son, that whoever believes in him should
not perish but have eternal life."

JOHN 3:16 ESV

BEAUTIFUL SAVIOR,

I long to comprehend the depth and breadth of *Your Love that surpasses knowledge*! I've seen that there's an enormous difference between really knowing You and simply knowing *about* You. Instead of just knowing some facts about You, I want to enjoy the glorious experience of Your loving Presence this Easter. I realize that I need the help of Your Spirit—*strengthening me with Power in my inner being so I can grasp how wide and long and high and deep is Your Love* for me.

You have been alive in my heart since the moment of my salvation. I've discovered that the more room I make for You in my inner being, the more You fill me with Your Love. You've been teaching me to expand this space in my heart by spending ample time with You and absorbing Your Word. I want to learn to stay in communication with You more and more—*praying continually.* These are joyful disciplines, and they keep me close to You.

Lord, I ask that Your Love may flow through me into the lives of other people. This *makes Your Love in me complete.*

IN YOUR LOVING NAME, JESUS, AMEN.

I have awakened in
your heart a strong
desire to know Me.
This longing originated
in Me, though it now
burns brightly in you.
When you seek My
Face in response to
My Love-call, both
of us are blessed.

I pray that out of his glorious riches he may strengthen you with power through his Spirit in your inner being, so that Christ may dwell in your hearts through faith. And I pray that you, being rooted and established in love, may have power . . . to grasp how wide and long and high and deep is the love of Christ.

Ephesians 3:16–18

Pray continually.

1 Thessalonians 5:17

No one has ever seen God; but if we love one another, God lives in us and his love is made complete in us.

1 John 4:12

MAJESTIC JESUS,

I come into Your Presence seeking rest and refreshment. Spending focused time with You strengthens and encourages me. Lord, I marvel at the wonder of communing with You—the Creator of the universe—while sitting in the comfort of my home.

Kings who reign on earth tend to make themselves inaccessible. Ordinary people almost never gain an audience with them. Even dignitaries must plow through red tape and protocol in order to speak with royalty. I rejoice that *You* are totally accessible to me—even though You are King of this vast, awesome universe.

Please help me remember that You are with me at all times and in all circumstances. *Nothing* can separate me from Your loving Presence! When You cried out from the cross, *"It is finished!" the curtain of the temple was torn in two from top to bottom*. This opened the way for me to meet You face to Face, with no need of protocol or priests. How breathtaking it is that You, *the King of kings*, are my constant Companion!

IN YOUR KINGLY NAME, AMEN.

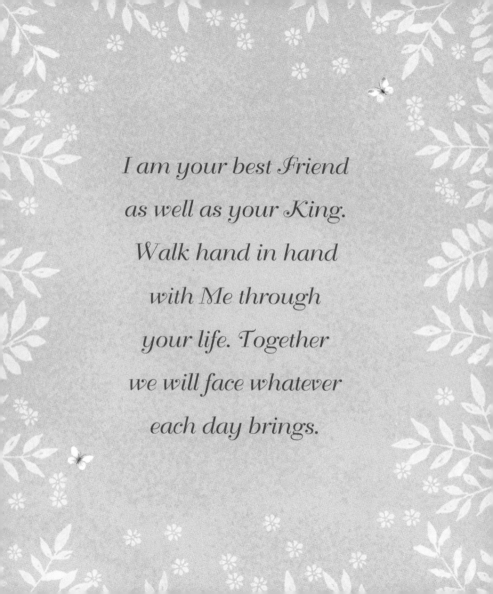

I am your best Friend

as well as your King.

Walk hand in hand

with Me through

your life. Together

we will face whatever

each day brings.

When Jesus had received the sour
wine, He said, "It is finished!"

JOHN 19:30 NKJV

When Jesus had cried out again in a loud
voice, he gave up his spirit. At that moment the
curtain of the temple was torn in two from top
to bottom. The earth shook and the rocks split.

MATTHEW 27:50–51

[The Lord Jesus Christ] is the blessed
and only Sovereign, the King of
kings, and the Lord of lords.

1 TIMOTHY 6:15 HCSB

MERCIFUL GOD,

I don't want to be *fearful of bad news*. Please help me to have *a steadfast heart, trusting in You*. In this world there is certainly an abundance of bad news. But instead of being afraid of what's happening, I want to rely confidently on You. Pondering Your sacrificial death on the cross and Your miraculous resurrection fills me with hope and gratitude. I rejoice that You, my living Savior, are Almighty God! And I find comfort in the truth that You are *sovereign* over global events—You are in control.

When things around me or things in the world look as if they're spinning out of control, I can come to You and *pour out my heart*. Instead of fretting and fuming, I can put that worry-energy into communicating with You.

Lord, I come to You not only for comfort but for direction. When I spend time waiting in Your Presence, You show me the right way to go.

Because I belong to You, I don't have to dread bad news or let it spook me. Instead, I can keep my heart steadfast and calm by boldly trusting in You.

IN YOUR STEADFAST NAME, JESUS, AMEN.

I crafted your mind for continual communication with Me. Bring Me all your needs, your hopes and fears. Commit everything into My care.

He will have no fear of bad news;
his heart is steadfast, trusting in the LORD.

PSALM 112:7

Yes, the Sovereign LORD is coming in power.
He will rule with a powerful arm. See, he
brings his reward with him as he comes.

ISAIAH 40:10 NLT

Trust in him at all times, O people; pour out
your hearts to him, for God is our refuge.

PSALM 62:8

WORTHY JESUS,

Help me to stay mindful of You as I go step by step through this day. Your Presence with me is a precious promise—and a comforting protection. After Your resurrection, You reassured Your followers, *"Surely I am with you always, to the very end of the age."* That promise was for *all* Your followers—including me!

While journeying with You, I've seen that Your Presence is a powerful, essential protection. As I walk along my life-path, there are numerous pitfalls nearby. Just a few steps away from my true path are pits of self-pity and despair, plateaus of pride and self-will. Various voices compete for my attention—trying to entice me to go their way. If I take my eyes off You and follow someone else's path, I am in real danger. I realize that even good friends can lead me astray if I let them usurp Your place in my life.

Thank You for showing me that the way to stay on *the path of Life* is to keep my focus on You. Awareness of Your loving Presence both protects me *and* delights me!

IN YOUR COMFORTING, PROTECTING NAME, AMEN.

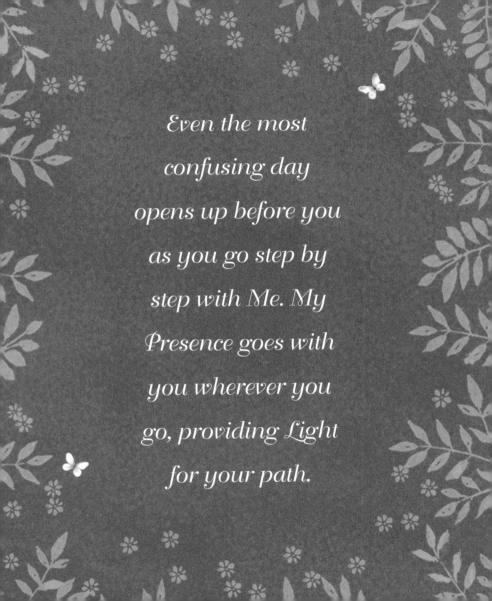

Even the most confusing day opens up before you as you go step by step with Me. My Presence goes with you wherever you go, providing Light for your path.

"Surely I am with you always, to
the very end of the age."

MATTHEW 28:20

Since we are surrounded by such a great cloud of
witnesses, let us throw off everything that hinders
and the sin that so easily entangles, and let us run
with perseverance the race marked out for us.

HEBREWS 12:1

You will show me the path of life; in Your
presence is fullness of joy; at Your right
hand are pleasures forevermore.

PSALM 16:11 NKJV

PRECIOUS LORD JESUS,

I love to hear You saying to me, *"I have called you by name; you are Mine!"* It's so comforting to know that I belong to You—no matter how isolated I sometimes feel. Thank You for redeeming me by paying the full penalty for my sins. I'm grateful that You called me to Yourself in the most personal way—reaching down into the circumstances of my life, speaking into the intricacies of my heart and mind. Even though You have vast numbers of followers, I am never just a number to You. You always speak to me *by name*. Scripture tells me I'm so precious to You that *You have inscribed me on the palms of Your hands. Nothing can separate me from Your loving Presence!*

When world events are swirling around me and my personal world feels unsteady, I don't want to let my thoughts linger on those stressors. Help me instead to focus my mind on the truth: Although this world is full of trouble, You are with me and You are in control. You're training me to change the subject from my problems to Your Presence by whispering, "But Jesus is with me" and then turning to You.

IN YOUR VICTORIOUS NAME, AMEN.

Be assured that I
never abandon any
of My children, not
even temporarily. I
will never leave you
or forsake you! My
Presence watches over
you continually.

This is what the Lord says, He who is your Creator, Jacob, and He who formed you, Israel: "Do not fear, for I have redeemed you; I have called you by name; you are Mine!"

ISAIAH 43:1 NASB

See, I have inscribed you on the palms of My hands; your walls are continually before Me.

ISAIAH 49:16 NKJV

Neither death nor life, neither angels nor demons, neither the present nor the future, nor any powers, neither height nor depth, nor anything else in all creation, will be able to separate us from the love of God that is in Christ Jesus our Lord.

ROMANS 8:38–39

REDEEMING SAVIOR,

I rejoice in You—knowing that Your sacrifice on the cross absorbed all my guilt: past, present, and future. *There is no condemnation for those who belong to You!*

My guilt-free status as Your child provides good reason to be joyful each day of my life. Ever since Adam and Eve's disobedience in the Garden of Eden, the world has been under the bondage of sin. I'm so grateful that Your sacrificial death provided the solution to this terrible problem. The gospel really is the best news imaginable! You took my sin—*You became sin for me*—and You gave me Your own perfect righteousness.

Please help me learn to fully enjoy my guilt-free status in Your kingdom. *Through You, the law of the Spirit of life has set me free.* I realize this is *not* an invitation to dive into a careless, sinful lifestyle. Instead, You enable me to live thankfully—celebrating the amazing privilege of belonging to You forever! It's such a wondrous blessing to know who I really am: a beloved *child of God.* This is my true identity, and it makes every moment of my life meaningful.

IN YOUR PRECIOUS NAME, JESUS, AMEN.

Trust Me enough
to accept the
full forgiveness
that I offer you
continually. This
great gift, which
cost Me My Life, is
yours for all eternity.

There is now no condemnation for those who are in Christ Jesus, because through Christ Jesus the law of the Spirit of life set me free from the law of sin and death.

ROMANS 8:1–2

He made Him who knew no sin to be sin for us, that we might become the righteousness of God in Him.

2 CORINTHIANS 5:21 NKJV

He came to his own, and his own people did not receive him. But to all who did receive him, who believed in his name, he gave the right to become children of God.

JOHN 1:11–12 ESV

My Savior-God,

I long for the absence of problems in my life, but I realize this is an unrealistic goal. Shortly before Your crucifixion, You told Your followers candidly: *"In this world you will have trouble."* I'm thankful I can look forward to an eternity of problem-free living, reserved for me in heaven. I rejoice in this glorious inheritance, which no one can take away from me. Teach me to wait patiently for this promised perfection rather than seeking my heaven here on earth.

Lord, help me to begin each day anticipating problems—asking You to equip me for whatever difficulties lie ahead. The best equipping is Your living Presence, Your hand that never lets go of mine.

Discussing my problems with You frees me to take a more lighthearted view of trouble—seeing it as a challenge that You and I together can handle. Please remind me again and again that You are on my side and *You have overcome the world!*

In Your conquering Name, Jesus, amen.

I am with you
continually, so don't
be intimidated by fear.
Though it stalks you,
it cannot harm you,
as long as you cling to
My hand. Keep your
eyes on Me, enjoying
Peace in My Presence.

"I have told you these things, so that in me you may have peace. In this world you will have trouble. But take heart! I have overcome the world."

JOHN 16:33

I am continually with You;
You hold me by my right hand.

PSALM 73:23 NKJV

What, then, shall we say in response to this?
If God is for us, who can be against us?

ROMANS 8:31

REJOICE

DELIGHTFUL JESUS,

Help me to *walk in the Light of Your Presence—acclaiming You, rejoicing in Your Name, and exulting in Your righteousness.* To acclaim You is to praise You in a strong and enthusiastic way, including shouts and applause. I rejoice in Your Name by delighting in all that You are—my Savior and Shepherd, my Lord and my God, my Sovereign King, my Friend who loves me with *unfailing Love.*

I exult in Your righteousness by reveling in the wondrous truth that You gave this priceless, holy gift to *me!* Your perfect righteousness is already credited to my account—even though I continue to battle sin in my life.

When I'm walking in Your glorious Light, *Your blood cleanses me from all sin.* As I seek to live near You, freely admitting I'm a sinner in need of forgiveness, Your radiant Presence purifies me. Moreover, this blessing of cleansing enables me to *have fellowship with* other believers.

Lord, I delight in walking in the Light with You—enjoying Your bright, loving Presence.

IN YOUR BRILLIANT NAME, AMEN.

Spend time
basking in the
Light of My
Presence. As you
come to know
Me more and
more intimately,
you grow
increasingly free.

Blessed are those who have learned to acclaim you, who walk in the light of your presence, O LORD. They rejoice in your name all day long; they exult in your righteousness.

PSALM 89:15–16

Let your face shine on your servant;
save me in your unfailing love.

PSALM 31:16

This righteousness from God comes through
faith in Jesus Christ to all who believe.

ROMANS 3:22

If we walk in the light as He is in the light, we
have fellowship with one another, and the blood of
Jesus Christ His Son cleanses us from all sin.

1 JOHN 1:7 NKJV

DEAREST JESUS,

You are worthy of all my confidence, all my trust! So instead of letting world events spook me, I'll pour my energy into trusting You and looking for evidence of Your Presence in the world. I love to whisper Your Name—to reconnect my heart and mind to You. *You are near to all who call upon You.* Please wrap me in Your abiding Presence and comfort me with Your Peace.

Help me remember that You are both loving and faithful. *Your Love reaches to the heavens, Your faithfulness to the skies.* This means that I can never come to the end of Your Love; it is limitless and everlasting! Moreover, I can stand on the Rock of Your faithfulness, no matter what circumstances I'm facing.

I realize that putting my confidence in my abilities, education, or success is futile and displeasing to You. Teach me to place my confidence fully in *You*—the Savior whose sacrificial death and miraculous resurrection opened the way for me into *eternal Glory*!

IN YOUR BREATHTAKING NAME, AMEN.

Having

sacrificed My

very Life for

you, I can be

trusted in every

facet of your life.

The LORD is near to all who call upon Him,
to all who call upon Him in truth.

PSALM 145:18 NKJV

Your love, O LORD, reaches to the heavens,
your faithfulness to the skies.

PSALM 36:5

Our light and momentary troubles are achieving for
us an eternal glory that far outweighs them all.

2 CORINTHIANS 4:17

COMPASSIONATE SAVIOR,

I *come to You* feeling *weary and burdened*, so I ask You to *give me rest*. Only You know the depth and breadth of my weariness. Nothing is hidden from You! You've been showing me that there's a time to keep pushing myself and there's a time to stop working—and just rest. Even You, who have infinite energy, rested on the seventh day after completing Your work of creation.

I want to spend time lingering in Your loving Presence while *Your Face shines upon me*. As favorite scriptures amble through my brain, they refresh my heart and spirit. When something comes to mind that I don't want to forget, I'll jot it down and then return my attention to You. As I'm relaxing with You, may Your Love soak into the depths of my being. I delight in expressing my love to *You*—in whispers, spoken words, and song.

Help me to believe that You approve of me and You approve of rest. While I relax in Your Presence, trusting in Your work on the cross, I am deeply refreshed.

IN YOUR INVIGORATING NAME, JESUS, AMEN.

As dew refreshes

grass and flowers

during the stillness

of the night, so My

Presence revitalizes

you as you sit

quietly with Me.

"Come to me, all you who are weary and burdened, and I will give you rest."

MATTHEW 11:28

On the seventh day God ended His work which He had done, and He rested on the seventh day.

GENESIS 2:2 NKJV

The LORD make His face shine upon you [with favor], and be gracious to you [surrounding you with lovingkindness]; the LORD lift up His countenance (face) upon you [with divine approval], and give you peace [a tranquil heart and life].

NUMBERS 6:25–26 AMP

My Savior-God,

I rejoice that Your *robe of righteousness* is mine eternally! Because You are my Savior forever, Your perfect righteousness can never be taken away from me. This means I don't need to be afraid of facing my sins—or dealing with them. As I become aware of sin in my life, I can confess it and receive Your forgiveness in full measure.

Help me also to forgive myself. I know that self-hatred is very unhealthy for me—and it is *not* pleasing to You. To avoid this hurtful snare, I'm learning to take many looks at *You* for every look I take at my sins and failures.

I delight in Your assurances that I am precious in Your sight. I'm so thankful I don't have to prove my worth by trying to be good enough. You lived a perfect life on my behalf because You knew I could not do so. Now I want to live in this glorious freedom of being Your fully forgiven follower—remembering that *there is no condemnation for those who belong to You*!

In Your forgiving Name, Jesus, amen.

My gaze upon you is steady and sure, untainted by sin. Through My eyes you can see yourself as one who is deeply, eternally loved. Rest in My loving gaze, and you will receive deep Peace. Respond to My loving Presence by worshiping Me in spirit and in truth.

My soul rejoices in my God. For he has . . .
arrayed me in a robe of righteousness.

ISAIAH 61:10

She will bring forth a Son, and you
shall call His name JESUS, for He will
save His people from their sins.

MATTHEW 1:21 NKJV

If we confess our sins, He is faithful and
just to forgive us our sins and to cleanse
us from all unrighteousness.

1 JOHN 1:9 NKJV

JESUS, MY PEACE,

You are *the Lord of Peace; You give Peace at all times and in every way*. There is a deep, gaping hole within me that can be filled only by Your peaceful Presence. Before I knew You, I tried to fill that emptiness in many different ways—or simply pretend it wasn't there. Even now, I often fail to recognize the full extent of my need for Your Peace at all times and in every situation. Moreover, You've been showing me that recognizing my neediness is only half the battle. The other half is to believe that You can—and will—*supply every need of mine*.

Shortly before Your death, You promised Peace to Your disciples—and to everyone who becomes Your follower. You made it clear that this is a gift, something You provide freely and lovingly. My part is just to *receive* this glorious gift—admitting my longing for it as well as my need. Please help me to wait patiently and expectantly in Your Presence, eager to receive Your Peace in full measure. I can express my openness to this gift by lifting my hands and saying, "Jesus, I receive Your Peace."

IN YOUR COMFORTING NAME, AMEN.

Peace be with you! Ever since the resurrection, this has been My watchword to those who yearn for Me. As you sit quietly, let My Peace settle over you and enfold you in My loving Presence.

Now may the Lord of peace himself
give you peace at all times and in every
way. The Lord be with all of you.

2 Thessalonians 3:16

My God will supply every need of yours
according to his riches in glory in Christ Jesus.

Philippians 4:19 esv

"Peace I leave with you, My peace I give to you;
not as the world gives do I give to you. Let not
your heart be troubled, neither let it be afraid."

John 14:27 nkjv

PRECIOUS JESUS,

I *rejoice that my name is written in heaven—in Your book of Life.* Because I am Yours, I have Joy that is independent of all circumstances. You have provided eternal Life that can *never* be taken away from me. Through faith in You as my risen Savior, I am *justified* and *also glorified.* Moreover, I have been *raised up with You and seated with You in the heavenly realms.*

Please help me remember that Joy is the birthright of all who belong to You, and it can coexist with the most difficult, painful circumstances. So I come to You this morning with open hands and open heart, saying, "Jesus, I receive Your Joy." While I wait with You, the Light of Your Presence shines upon me—soaking into the depths of my inner being. Thus You strengthen me, preparing me for the day that stretches out before me.

I'm grateful that I can return to You for fresh supplies of Joy as often as I need. Since You are a God of limitless abundance, You always have more than enough for me!

IN YOUR BOUNTIFUL NAME, AMEN.

I am a God who gives and gives and gives. When I died for you on the cross, I held back nothing; I poured out My Life like a drink offering. Because giving is inherent in My nature, I search for people who are able to receive in full measure.

"Rejoice that your names are written in heaven."

Luke 10:20

Nothing unclean will ever enter it, nor anyone who
does what is detestable or false, but only those
who are written in the Lamb's book of life.

Revelation 21:27 esv

Those He called, He also justified; and
those He justified, He also glorified.

Romans 8:30 hcsb

God raised us up with Christ and seated us with
him in the heavenly realms in Christ Jesus.

Ephesians 2:6

TREASURED LORD JESUS,

Help me to trust in *Your unfailing Love*—thanking You for the good I cannot see. When evil seems to be flourishing in the world around me, it feels as if things are spinning out of control. But I know *You* are not wringing Your hands helplessly, wondering what to do next. As Your resurrection proved, You are completely in control, working behind-the-scenes goodness in the midst of the turmoil. So, in faith, I thank You not only for the blessings I can see but for the ones I can't see.

Your *wisdom and knowledge* are deeper and richer than my words could ever express. *Your judgments are unsearchable, and Your paths beyond tracing out!* So my wisest choice is to *trust in You at all times*—even when my world feels unsteady and I don't understand Your ways.

I need to remember that *You are always with me, holding me by my right hand. And afterward You will take me into Glory.* As I ponder this hidden treasure—my heavenly inheritance—I thank You for this glorious blessing I cannot yet see!

IN YOUR SACRED NAME, AMEN.

Though the world around you is messy and confusing, remember that I have overcome the world. I have told you these things so that in Me you may have Peace.

"Though the mountains be shaken and the hills be removed, yet my unfailing love for you will not be shaken nor my covenant of peace be removed," says the LORD, who has compassion on you.

ISAIAH 54:10

Oh, the depth of the riches of the wisdom and knowledge of God! How unsearchable his judgments, and his paths beyond tracing out!

ROMANS 11:33

I am always with you; you hold me by my right hand. You guide me with your counsel, and afterward you will take me into glory.

PSALM 73:23—24

GRACIOUS GOD,

Sometimes I hear You whispering in my heart, *"I take great delight in you."* It's hard for me to receive this blessing, but I know it's based on the unconditional Love You have for all Your children. Please help me to relax in the Light of Your Presence—taking time to soak in Your luminous Love. I long to sit quietly with You while You *renew me by Your Love.*

I find it terribly challenging to live in a fallen world. There is so much brokenness all around me as well as within me. But I can choose—moment by moment—to focus on what is wrong or to *seek Your Face* and enjoy your approval.

I need to remember that Your delight in me is based on Your work on the cross. This remembrance protects me from falling into the trap of trying to earn Your Love. Teach me to live as the one I truly am—Your beloved child, *saved by grace through faith.* Then my gratitude will keep me close to You, eager to follow wherever You lead.

IN YOUR WONDROUS NAME, JESUS, AMEN.

In the Light of
My Love, you are
gradually transformed
from glory to glory. It
is through spending
time with Me that
you realize how
wide and long and
high and deep is
My Love for you.

The LORD your God is in your midst; he is a warrior who can deliver. He takes great delight in you; he renews you by his love; he shouts for joy over you.

ZEPHANIAH 3:17 NET

When You said, "Seek My face," my heart said to You, "Your face, LORD, I will seek."

PSALM 27:8 NKJV

You are saved by grace through faith, and this is not from yourselves; it is God's gift.

EPHESIANS 2:8 HCSB

PRECIOUS JESUS,

Help me to find Joy even in the most unlikely places. I know this requires effort on my part—searching for the good and refusing to let my natural responses blind me to what is there. Please open my eyes to see beyond the obvious so that I can discover treasures hidden in my troubles.

You've been teaching me that living joyously is a choice. Because I inhabit such a sinful, broken world, I must make the effort to choose gladness many times a day. This is especially true during my difficult times. Your Word tells me to *consider it pure joy whenever I face trials of many kinds*. This verse shows me that when I encounter various difficulties, I'm being put to the test. Such trials can strengthen my faith—which is *much more precious than gold*—and prove that it is genuine.

Thank You, Jesus, for making the excruciating decision to *endure the cross for the Joy set before You*—the eternal pleasure of *bringing many sons and daughters to Glory*. Please enable me to choose Joy by *fixing my eyes on You* and looking for treasures in my trials.

IN YOUR COURAGEOUS NAME, AMEN.

Though I pour out blessings upon you always, some of My richest blessings have to be actively sought. I love to reveal Myself to you, and your seeking heart opens you up to receive more of My disclosure.

Consider it pure joy . . . whenever you face trials
of many kinds, because you know that the testing
of your faith develops perseverance.

JAMES 1:2–3

In this you greatly rejoice . . . that the genuineness of
your faith, being much more precious than gold that
perishes, though it is tested by fire, may be found to praise,
honor, and glory at the revelation of Jesus Christ.

1 PETER 1:6–7 NKJV

Let us fix our eyes on Jesus, the author and perfecter of our
faith, who for the joy set before him endured the cross.

HEBREWS 12:2

In bringing many sons to glory, it was fitting that God . . . should
make the author of their salvation perfect through suffering.

HEBREWS 2:10

BELOVED JESUS,

Your Word tells me that *You call me by name and You lead me. You know me*—You know every detail about me! I am never a number or statistic to You. Your involvement in my life is wonderfully personal and intimate. I love to hear You whisper in my heart: "Beloved, *follow Me.*"

After Your resurrection, when Mary Magdalene mistook You for the gardener, You spoke just one word to her: *"Mary."* Hearing You say her name, she recognized You at once and *cried out in Aramaic, "Rabboni!" (Teacher).*

Because I am Your follower, You also speak *my* name—in the depths of my spirit. When I take time to hear You speaking to me personally in Scripture, reassuring me of Your Love, I am blessed. I delight in these beautiful words of blessing: *I called you out of darkness into My marvelous Light*, and *I have loved you with an everlasting Love*. The unshakable knowledge that You love me forever provides a firm foundation for my life. Help me to follow You faithfully and joyfully—*proclaiming Your praises* as I journey through my life.

IN YOUR MAGNIFICENT NAME, AMEN.

I speak to you

from the depths

of your being.

Hear Me saying

soothing words of

Peace, assuring

you of My Love.

"He calls his own sheep by name and leads
them out. . . . My sheep listen to my voice;
I know them, and they follow me."

JOHN 10:3, 27

Jesus said to her, "Mary." She turned toward him and cried
out in Aramaic, "Rabboni!" (which means Teacher).

JOHN 20:16

You are a chosen generation . . . His own special
people, that you may proclaim the praises of Him who
called you out of darkness into His marvelous light.

1 PETER 2:9 NKJV

"I have loved you with an everlasting love; therefore
with lovingkindness I have drawn you."

JEREMIAH 31:3 NKJV

MY LIVING LORD,

I rejoice that *You are the living One who sees me*. You are far more fully, gloriously alive than I can begin to imagine. When I see You *face to Face* in all Your Glory, I know I will be awestruck! Now, though, *I see in a mirror dimly*. My view of You is obscured by my fallen condition.

It's wonderful—and rather daunting—that You see *me* with perfect clarity. You know everything about me, including my most secret thoughts and feelings. You understand how broken and weak I am: *You remember that I am dust*. But in spite of all my flaws and failures, You choose to love me with everlasting Love.

Help me to remember that the gift of Your Love was immeasurably costly. You endured unspeakable agony to save me from my sins. You *became sin for me so that I might become righteous in You*. I love to ponder this wondrous truth: Your perfect righteousness has been credited to me forever! This gift of infinite value has been mine ever since I trusted You as my Savior. I'm so thankful that *the living One who sees me* always is the same One who loves me eternally!

IN YOUR SAVING NAME, JESUS, AMEN.

I have gifted you with
fragility, providing
opportunities for your spirit
to blossom in My Presence.
Accept this gift as a sacred
treasure: delicate yet
glowing with brilliant Light.
Rather than struggling
to disguise or deny your
weakness, allow Me to bless
you richly through it.

The well was called Beer-lahai-roi [A well to the Living One Who sees me].

GENESIS 16:14 AMPC

For now we see in a mirror dimly, but then face to face. Now I know in part; then I shall know fully, even as I have been fully known.

1 CORINTHIANS 13:12 ESV

He knows our frame;
He remembers that we are dust.

PSALM 103:14 NKJV

Loving Savior,

You brought me out into a spacious place. You rescued me because You delighted in me. I know that Your delight in me wasn't based on any worthiness that was in me. You freely *chose* to lavish Your Love on me—bringing me out of *slavery to sin* into a spacious place of salvation. Since my best efforts were utterly insufficient to save myself, *You rescued me* and clothed me in Your own perfect righteousness. Help me to wear this *clothing of salvation* with overflowing Joy—*living as a child of Light,* secure in Your radiant righteousness.

Salvation is the greatest, most precious gift I could ever receive, and I'll never stop thanking You for it! In the morning when I awake, I'll rejoice that You have adopted me into Your royal family. Before I go to sleep at night, I'll praise You for Your glorious grace.

Lord, I want to live in ways that help other people see *You* as the Source of abundant, never-ending Life!

In Your righteous, royal Name, Jesus, amen.

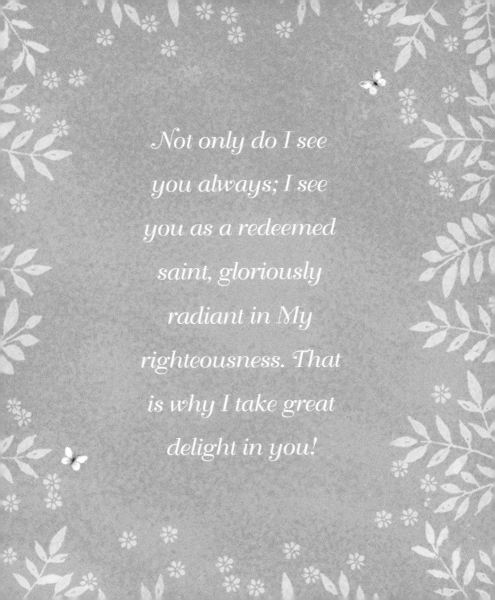

Not only do I see you always; I see you as a redeemed saint, gloriously radiant in My righteousness. That is why I take great delight in you!

He brought me out into a spacious place;
he rescued me because he delighted in me.

PSALM 18:19

Jesus replied, "I tell you the truth, everyone
who sins is a slave to sin."

JOHN 8:34

I am overwhelmed with joy in the LORD my God! For
he has dressed me with the clothing of salvation.

ISAIAH 61:10 NLT

You were once darkness, but now you are light
in the Lord. Live as children of light.

EPHESIANS 5:8

My living Savior,

Your Word shows me that it's possible for Your followers to be joyful and afraid at the same time. When an angel told the women who came to Your tomb that You had risen from the dead, they were *afraid yet filled with Joy.* So I don't have to let fear keep me from experiencing the Joy of Your Presence. This pleasure is not a luxury reserved for times when my problems—and the crises in the world—seem under control. Your loving Presence is mine to enjoy today, tomorrow, and forever!

Lord, help me not to give in to joyless living by letting worries about the present or the future weigh me down. Instead, I need to remember that *neither the present nor the future, nor any powers, neither height nor depth, nor anything else in all creation, will be able to separate me from Your Love.*

I'm thankful that I can talk freely with You about my fears, expressing my thoughts and feelings candidly. As I relax in Your Presence and entrust all my concerns to You, please bless me with Your Joy—*which no one can take away from me.*

In Your delightful Name, Jesus, amen.

Ask My Spirit to

live through you, as

you wend your way

through this day.

Hold My hand in

joyful trust, for I never

leave your side.

The women hurried away from the tomb, afraid
yet filled with joy, and ran to tell his disciples.

MATTHEW 28:8

I am convinced that . . . neither the present nor the
future, nor any powers, neither height nor depth, nor
anything else in all creation, will be able to separate us
from the love of God that is in Christ Jesus our Lord.

ROMANS 8:38–39

"You too have grief now; but I will see you
again, and your heart will rejoice, and no
one will take your joy away from you."

JOHN 16:22 NASB 1995

Beloved Jesus,

I want to live in continual awareness of Your Presence and Your Peace. I know that these are gifts of supernatural proportions. Ever since Your resurrection, You have comforted Your followers with these wonderful messages: *"Surely I am with you always"* and *"Peace be with you."* Please help me to be increasingly receptive to You, Lord, as You offer me these glorious gifts. I'm learning that the best way to receive Your Presence and Peace is to thank You for them.

I am delighted that You created me first and foremost to glorify You. This means it's impossible for me to spend too much time thanking and praising You. I've found that thanksgiving and praise put me in proper relationship with You—opening the way for Your Joy to flow into me as I draw near You in worship.

Thanking You for Your Presence and Your Peace is a wise investment of time, enabling me to receive more of You and Your precious gifts.

In Your glorious Name, amen.

Do not hesitate to receive Joy from Me, for I bestow it on you abundantly. The more you rest in My Presence, the more freely My blessings flow into you.

While they were still talking about this,
Jesus himself stood among them and
said to them, "Peace be with you."

LUKE 24:36

Through Jesus, therefore, let us continually
offer to God a sacrifice of praise—the
fruit of lips that confess his name.

HEBREWS 13:15

Thanks be to God for His indescribable gift!

2 CORINTHIANS 9:15 NKJV

My risen Savior,

I'm so thankful that *You have given me new birth into a living hope through Your resurrection from the dead*! Moreover, *I am a new creation; the old has gone, the new has come!*

My adoption into Your royal family occurred the moment I first trusted You as my Savior-God. At that instant, my spiritual status changed from death to life—eternal Life. I have *an inheritance that can never perish, spoil, or fade—kept in heaven for me.* My heart overflows with gratefulness for Your provision of this glorious inheritance!

You've shown me that even though I'm *a new creation,* my conversion was only the beginning of the work Your Spirit is doing in me. I need *to be made new in the attitude of my mind and to put on the new self*—becoming increasingly righteous and holy. This strenuous, marvelous, lifelong endeavor is preparing me to spend an eternity with You in Glory! Please help me to receive this assignment with courage and gratitude—staying alert and looking for all the wonderful things You are doing in my life.

In Your magnificent Name, Jesus, amen.

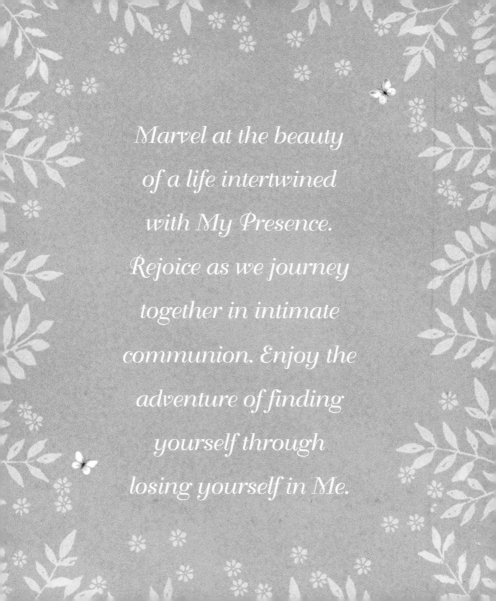

Marvel at the beauty
of a life intertwined
with My Presence.
Rejoice as we journey
together in intimate
communion. Enjoy the
adventure of finding
yourself through
losing yourself in Me.

In his great mercy [God] has given us new birth into
a living hope through the resurrection of Jesus Christ
from the dead, and into an inheritance that can never
perish, spoil or fade—kept in heaven for you.

1 PETER 1:3–4

If anyone is in Christ, he is a new creation;
the old has gone, the new has come!

2 CORINTHIANS 5:17

Just as Christ was raised from the dead by the glory of the
Father, even so we also should walk in newness of life.

ROMANS 6:4 NKJV

DEAR JESUS,

You are the Risen One—my *living God*. I celebrate the Joy of serving a Savior who is so exuberantly alive! I rejoice also in Your promise to be with me continually—throughout time and eternity. These truths can sustain me through my worst trials and deepest disappointments. So help me to walk boldly with You along the path of Life, trusting confidently that You will never let go of my hand.

I delight in thinking about all that You offer me: Your loving Presence, complete forgiveness of my sins, and forever-pleasures in heaven. This is all so extravagant and lavish that I can't even begin to comprehend it! That is why worshiping You is so important to me. It's a powerful way of connecting with You that transcends my ever-so-limited understanding.

I enjoy worshiping You in a variety of ways—singing hymns and praise songs, studying and memorizing Your Word, praying individually and with others, glorying in the wonders of Your creation. Another way I worship You is by serving others and loving them with Your Love. *Whatever I do*, Lord, I want to *do it all for Your Glory*!

IN YOUR VICTORIOUS NAME, AMEN.

I created mankind to

glorify Me and enjoy

Me forever. I provide

the Joy; your part

is to glorify Me by

living close to Me.

The angel said to the women, "Do not be afraid, for I know that you are looking for Jesus, who was crucified. He is not here; he has risen, just as he said."

MATTHEW 28:5–6

My soul thirsts for God, for the living God. When can I go and meet with God?

PSALM 42:2

All the treasures of wisdom and knowledge are hidden in Him.

COLOSSIANS 2:3 HCSB

Whether you eat or drink or whatever you do, do it all for the glory of God.

1 CORINTHIANS 10:31

My Easter Prayers

My Easter Prayers

About the Author

Sarah Young, author of the bestselling 365-day devotionals *Jesus Calling*® and *Jesus Listens*, was a missionary alongside her husband, Stephen, for forty-five years. In her writing and in her mission work, Sarah was committed to helping people connect with Jesus and the Bible. Her books have sold more than 45 million copies worldwide. *Jesus Calling*® has appeared on all major bestseller lists. Sarah's writings include *Jesus Calling*®, *Jesus Listens*, *Jesus Always*, *Jesus Today*®, *Jesus Lives*™, *Dear Jesus*, *Jesus Calling*® *for Little Ones*, *Jesus Calling*® *Bible Storybook*, *Jesus Calling*®: *365 Devotions for Kids*, and more, each encouraging readers in their journeys toward intimacy with Christ. Sarah believed that praying for her readers was a privilege and God-given responsibility and did so daily even amid her own health challenges.

Connect with Jesus Calling at:
Facebook.com/JesusCalling
Instagram.com/JesusCalling
YouTube.com/JesusCallingBook
Pinterest.com/Jesus_Calling

Experience Peace
in His Presence

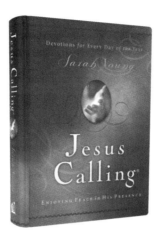

Written as if Jesus Himself is speaking directly
to you—words of encouragement, comfort,
and reassurance of His unending love.

Jesus Calling® is your yearlong guide to living a more
peaceful life, delivering His message of love every day.

ISBN 978-1-5914-5188-4

I AM THE GIFT that continuously gives—bounteously, with no strings attached. Unconditional Love is such a radical concept that even My most devoted followers fail to grasp it fully. Absolutely nothing in heaven or on earth can cause Me to stop loving you.

—AN EXCERPT FROM *JESUS CALLING*®

Easter Has Always
Been Part of God's Story

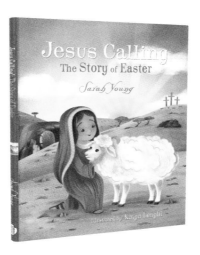

Jesus Calling®: The Story of Easter, from bestselling
author Sarah Young, uses storytelling from
throughout the Bible, simple Bible verses, and short
Jesus Calling® devotions to show kids how Easter
was part of God's plan from the very beginning.

ISBN 978-1-4002-1032-9

In the beginning, before anything was created, there was God.

And God had a beautiful plan.

He hung stars in the sky and set the earth in its place.

Flowers bloomed, fish splashed, and birds soared.

Animals of every kind crawled and ran and hopped.

And He made people too.

God gave His creation everything it needed. And when His people needed someone to save them, He would send Jesus, His very own Son.

That was the beginning of Easter.

—AN EXCERPT FROM *JESUS CALLING®: THE STORY OF EASTER*

Help Your Kids Discover
How to Talk to God

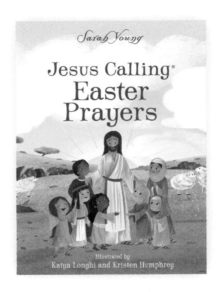

Invite your children to join the celebration of
Jesus' resurrection and learn to pray with this
Easter read-aloud children's book by Sarah
Young, bestselling author of *Jesus Calling*®.

ISBN 978-1-4002-3446-2